THE SCARIEST PLACES ON EARTH

PARIS CATACOMBS

BY DENNY VON FINN

BELLWETHER MEDIA · MINNEAPOLIS, MN

Are you ready to take it to the extreme?
Torque books thrust you into the action-packed world
of sports, vehicles, mystery, and adventure. These
books may include dirt, smoke, fire, and chilling tales.
WARNING : read at your own risk.

Library of Congress Cataloging-in-Publication Data

Von Finn, Denny.
Paris Catacombs / by Denny Von Finn.
    pages cm. -- (Torque : the scariest places on earth)
Includes bibliographical references and index.
Summary: "Engaging images accompany information about the Paris Catacombs. The combination of
high-interest subject matter and light text is intended for students in grades 3 through 7"--Provided by
publisher.
ISBN 978-1-60014-949-8 (hardcover : alk. paper)
1. Catacombs--France--Paris--Juvenile literature. 2. Cemeteries--France--Paris--History--Juvenile literature.
3. Underground areas--France--Paris--Juvenile literature. I. Title.
DC753.V66 2014
944'.361--dc23
                                                    2013007959

This edition first published in 2014 by Bellwether Media, Inc.

Printed in the United States of America, North Mankato, MN.

TABLE OF CONTENTS

CHAPTER 1

THE EMPIRE OF DEATH

Damp gravel crunches beneath your sneakers. Lightbulbs flicker overhead. Your eyes slowly adjust to the underground darkness.

You tiptoe around a corner. There is a door with a sign above it. The sign reads, "Stop! Here lies the **empire** of death."

ARRÊTE!
C'EST ICI L'EMPIRE DE LA MOR

WHAT DOES IT MEAN?

The word *catacomb* comes from a Latin phrase that means "among the tombs."

OSSEMENS DE L'ÉGLISE
ET DU CLOÎTRE DES
CAPUCINS S. HONORÉ
LE 29 MARS 1804

You look over your shoulder. Then, you step through the doorway. You cannot believe what you see! Thousands of bones line the walls. They are arranged in neat rows. Some even make patterns. The sight sends a shiver up your spine. Welcome to the Paris **catacombs**.

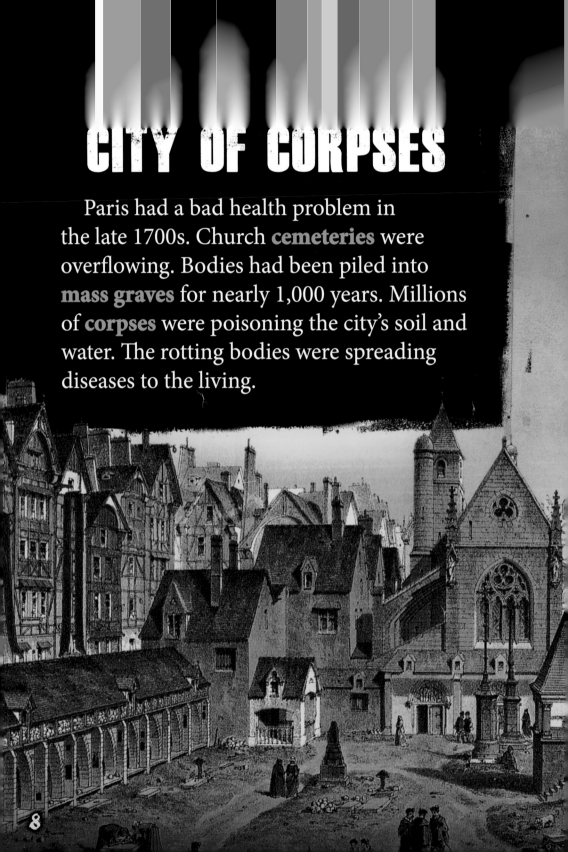

CITY OF CORPSES

Paris had a bad health problem in the late 1700s. Church **cemeteries** were overflowing. Bodies had been piled into **mass graves** for nearly 1,000 years. Millions of **corpses** were poisoning the city's soil and water. The rotting bodies were spreading diseases to the living.

TOWER OF TERROR

Some say the earth covering the dead at one cemetery rose more than 10 feet (3 meters) above the street!

Police officer Alexandre Lenoir had an idea. The city could move the bones of rotted corpses to the city's **quarries**. These were long, maze-like tunnels beneath the city. They had been dug to remove stone that was used to construct the great buildings in Paris.

AROUND THE WORLD
Italy, Egypt, and Peru are also home to famous catacombs.

11

Workers began to remove the bones from cemeteries in 1786. They worked only at night. They tossed the rattling bones down a hole into the quarries.

The bones quickly piled up. Louis-Étienne Héricart de Thury began to arrange them in interesting patterns. He and his workers formed hearts, crosses, and other shapes with the bones.

The bone-filled quarries became known as the catacombs. Bones were brought there until 1859. They belonged to the bodies of more than 6 million people. Some believe that the spirits of their owners are angry. Their bones have been put on display for the living to see!

THE SECOND CITY

About 2 million people live in the city of Paris. There are more than twice as many dead Parisians in the catacombs!

CHAPTER 3
MORE THAN BONES?

The old quarries beneath Paris stretch at least 180 miles (290 kilometers). The catacombs are just a small part of the tunnels. Thousands of **tourists** visit them each year.

Some people are even more daring. **Cataphiles** explore parts of the tunnels that are not open to visitors. This may not be wise. Who knows where they might end up? What if they cannot find the way back out?

tomb of Philibert Aspairt

A LA MÉMOIRE
DE PHILIBERT ASPAIRT
PERDU DANS CETTE
CARRIÈRE LE III NOV^BRE
MDCCXCIII RETROUVÉ
ONZE ANS APRÈS ET
INHUMÉ EN LA MÊME PLACE
LE XXX AVRIL MDCCCIV

A DARK END

A man named Philibert Aspairt is said to have gotten lost in the catacombs in 1793. His body was found eleven years later. It was lying just feet from an exit. Today, his tomb rests in the spot where his body was found.

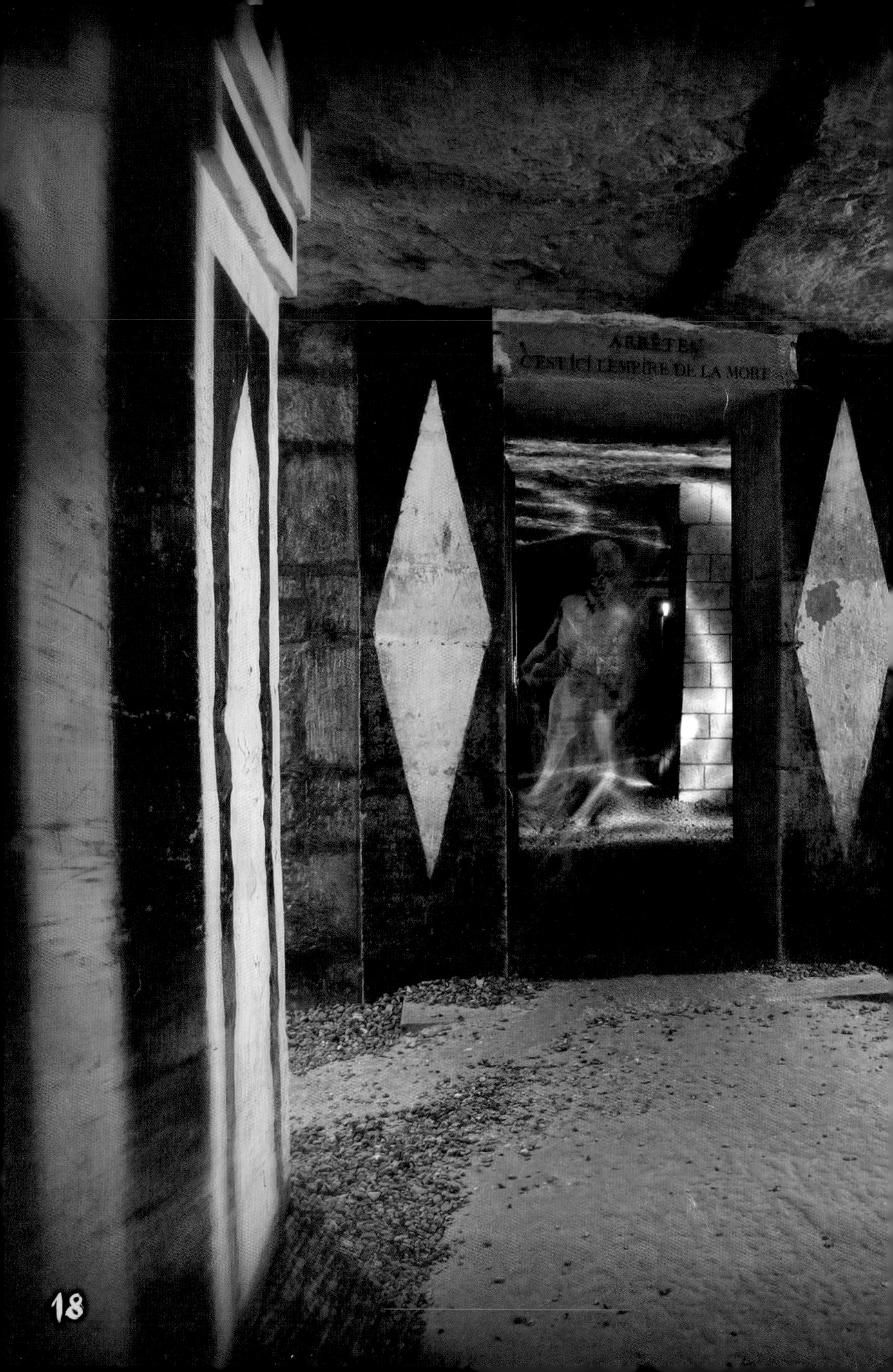
ARRÊTEZ!
C'EST ICI L'EMPIRE DE LA MORT

Most catacomb visitors bring cameras. Some have later noticed cloudy shapes in their photos and videos. Were these ghost-like mists following the visitors? Some people have felt the touch of a hand when no one was near. A few have even felt like they were being strangled.

GOING DOWN

Visitors climb down 130 stone steps to the catacomb floor. That is 66 feet (20 meters) below the street!

Ghost hunters have taken an interest in the Paris catacombs. Some have made **EVP** recordings. These sounds are not heard at the time of recording. Researchers pick them up when the tape is played back.

Could these **eerie** sounds be the crying spirits of the dead? If so, what do they want? Perhaps the spirits are angry at being forgotten. Or maybe they just want to rest in peace.

GLOSSARY

catacombs—underground tombs

cataphiles—people who explore the Paris catacombs for fun

cemeteries—places where the dead are buried

corpses—dead bodies

eerie—strange and scary

empire—a kingdom or territory under one ruling body

EVP—electronic voice phenomena; EVP recordings sound like speech but have no known source.

mass graves—large holes in which many corpses are buried

quarries—underground pits from which stone is taken

tourists—people who travel to visit another place

TO LEARN MORE

AT THE LIBRARY

Gee, Joshua. *Encyclopedia Horrifica*. New York, N.Y.: Scholastic Inc., 2007.

Goodman, Michael E. *Dark Labyrinths*. New York, N.Y.: Bearport Pub., 2010.

Whiting, Jim. *Scary Ghosts*. Mankato, Minn.: Capstone Press, 2010.

ON THE WEB

Learning more about the Paris Catacombs is as easy as 1, 2, 3.

1. Go to www.factsurfer.com.

2. Enter "Paris Catacombs" into the search box.

3. Click the "Surf" button and you will see a list of related Web sites.

With factsurfer.com, finding more information is just a click away.

INDEX